MY 365 IN 30 DAYS

D1262229

NEISHA O CAVE

My 365 In 30 Days

ISBN: 9798655814660 (Paperback)

Disclaimer: The author makes no guarantees concerning the level of success you may experience by following the advice and strategies contained in this book. It is intended for motivational purposes and provides a source of valuable information for the reader.

This book is dedicated to HER.

She was abrasive because she unaware of her power
and true potential.

Now she is growing and glowing because she's woke.

People feared her while she was afraid of her own potential.

They tried to keep her quiet but somehow she was always
the loudest in the room.

Her name has kissed the walls of so many rooms that
her feet has never ventured.

Appreciate her rebirth.

All it took was 30 days,

Now she is courageous but humble and ready to conquer!

ACKNOWLEDGEMENT

To give acknowledgment is to recognize that "No man is an island". I want to thank God for blessing me with the spirit of dedication, commitment, and strong-will. He gave me two angels to accompany me in all my adventures, Kelly-Ann and Tiffany, I feel their spirits guiding me. I have arrived at such a great point in my journey! When I decided to birth this project, the morals and standards that Vernella and Samuel instilled in me came to the forefront. I wish to express my appreciation for my dear aunt Delorse for all your hard work, I hope I've made you proud. My gratitude for my entire publishing team is unprecedented and for you, I am truly honored. Thank you to all the soldiers in my camp, we fought a great fight.

I salute you with purple love!

INTRODUCTION- THE BUTTERFLY

When I decided to birth this project, I had just gone through a very difficult period in my life. The scary part of it all was that I somehow found time to uplift everyone around me. I was a year and a half deep into what I considered to be mental suicide because I felt like a noose was tied around the neck of my aspirations and goals. I must admit, it wasn't intentional but it felt very deliberate. By this time, theoretically, I was supposed to be settled and ready to give this new life a try. I was a bright-eyed, bushy-tailed economist whose job description could be summarised as "sales-woman". During this time, whenever I failed I would make excuses. This could not be my fault! But I took full responsibility for this one. This one was all me. I was living in survival mode and I felt like I was drowning.

On the surface, I packaged it well with non-designer clothes and 4" Aldo heels. I am sure when you read this, if you ever do, I am sounding like a hypocrite but I promise you that's not the case. I was not struggling to pay my bills, work was a stones-throw away from my apartment, my family was supportive and people loved me even when I struggled to love myself. Still, I was unhappy and disgusted with the sight of my growth or lack thereof. I felt vulnerable, out of place, and trapped in so many situations that I lost count of the different versions of Neisha Cave.

During several interviews, I battled with the question "Who is Neisha Cave?" because I wasn't sure anymore. I even made commitments that I knew were unattainable because my mind was poisoned by doubt and fear. My mind was racing and I just couldn't catch up, but then one day I felt a shift. It was a sudden shift, an eruption caused by constant friction. It was the breakthrough that shattered all my self-doubts and negative thoughts.

My rebirth came without warning or instruction, I was no longer in survival mode because I was happily living! The most interesting aspect of this story is that I adjusted my mindset and the way I dealt with unfavorable situations. That occurred and little did I know half the battle was won. I was so engulfed in the new thought process that I didn't even realize when it changed. You see, when you are laser-focused the world will be changing and so will you. I felt like I had finally found the tanzanite that I needed to show up and show off. I realized that the breakthrough was just the beginning of my rebirth and it was time to consistently have a positive mindset that would carry me through this journey called life.

La Mariposa

Luckily for you, you don't have to figure it out on your own. This 30-day motivational program gives you the tools that are necessary to shift a negative mindset and prepare you for a life of greatness and prosperity.

DAY 1

The beginning of your 365 (year) starts right now!

Let's get one thing clear, You have full control over your day, week, month, year, and most importantly YOUR LIFE. Sometimes we become so obsessed with a new year's resolution but by mid-Jan, we already forgot what we would've resolved to achieve. I, Your Name have declared that the birth and berth of my year is dd/mm/yy. Your year or rebirth begins when you decide to make a change in your life rather than by a government's calendar.

You give birth where the water breaks!

Today's Affirmation:

_____

_____

_____

_____

_____

_____

_____

_____

Evening Reflection:

_____

_____

_____

_____

_____

_____

_____

_____

_____

DAY 2

I have determined what's good for my soul and happiness is paramount. From today onward I will reject anything that doesn't feed my soul.

Become very selfish with your energy! Don't allow everyone to have access to you and your energy. Unplug, take a break and remove yourself from toxic relationships and environments if you must. Your energy is a great dictator of your view of the world and therefore you must keep it sacred.

Treat your soul with positivity and prosperity and everything you touch will evolve to Gold!

Today's Affirmation:

_____

_____

_____

_____

_____

_____

_____

_____

_____

_____

Evening Reflection:

_____

_____

_____

_____

_____

_____

_____

_____

_____

_____

DAY 3

*This is your year of births; You will transform
your concepts into conceptions.*

Get out of your head, get in the race, and stay in your lane. Remember those concepts were given to you by God to innovate and enrich the lives of others. Stop spending so much time wishing you "could have" or being scared that people won't like your idea. It takes courage to act on behalf of what you see and feel on the inside. It's in your DNA to be extraordinary; just command and commit to your ideas and watch them birth right before your eyes.

Oh, what power God has given you, to create!

Today's Affirmation:

_____

_____

_____

_____

_____

_____

_____

_____

_____

Evening Reflection:

_____

_____

_____

_____

_____

_____

_____

_____

_____

DAY 4

You are the master of your own destiny when you can be alone without being lonely.

This quote was written well before the COVID-19 Pandemic and it became even more timely during that period because so many of us felt the wrath of isolation. We didn't have to find the time to be alone with our thoughts and feelings, we were forced to. This was the period to authentically feel. If we spend all our time in other people's company, we aren't allowing our spirit to be genuinely happy, hurt, or heal. When the universe forces you to come to a complete halt it's only then you realize you were lost all along. Make room for alone time so you can master your destiny.

I really want to rule my destiny - Buju Banton

Today's Affirmation:

_____

_____

_____

_____

_____

_____

_____

_____

_____

_____

Evening Reflection:

_____

_____

_____

_____

_____

_____

_____

_____

_____

_____

DAY 5

Don't give them what they want. Starve the demon!

Distractions! They are the ultimate blindside leading to that outcome called failure. When you become so invested in the wrong people and the wrong things this causes you to lose sight of your own goals. Don't allow friends, family, relationships, and/ or workplaces stresses to stunt your growth. Engage in feeding your goals and dreams and starve the demon of distraction. You owe it to yourself to be disciplined and discard your inhibitions.

Fill your cup!

Today's Affirmation:

_____

_____

_____

_____

_____

_____

_____

_____

_____

Evening Reflection:

_____

_____

_____

_____

_____

_____

_____

_____

_____

_____

DAY 6

*We are all guilty of putting others first but we
are about to change the game!*

You cannot be helpful or meaningful to others if you are ripped into several pieces, you have to be whole to be wholesome to others. Practice self-love, self-care, and selfishness and by all means embrace being SELF-FULL. Become so full that anything you share with others is simply an overflow instead of diluting the essence of your happiness. Ask yourself these three (3) questions:

- Do I have enough to share?
- Have I robbed myself?
- How swiftly can I replenish/replace it?

I am me because no one else can be, so I have to preserve me!

Today's Affirmation:

_____

_____

_____

_____

_____

_____

_____

_____

_____

Evening Reflection:

_____

_____

_____

_____

_____

_____

_____

_____

_____

DAY 7

Nurture your mind to mentally remove all limits and make grand accomplishments before you arrive. Your arrival will be the final step.

Your parents may have failed! Their parents may have failed! You will NOT fail! You will break the generational curse that's expected to run through your bones like DNA. Trust me when I say that others are looking up to you, cheering and praying that you can break the curse and clear the path for the youngster. You won't fail because here is a list of your intangible inheritance:

1. Strength of a Herd of Oxen
2. Wisdom of a Parliament of Owls
3. Endurance of a Herd of Stallions

Your success is only as good as your mentality, so remember to update your default settings to change your mindset! -T D Jakes

Today's Affirmation:

_____

_____

_____

_____

_____

_____

_____

_____

Evening Reflection:

_____

_____

_____

_____

_____

_____

_____

_____

DAY 8

Speak life and positivity into everything you do!

Breathing can be defined as the way you think and speak about your goals and dreams. The tongue is so powerful, that you can declare failure into your life before you even lift a finger. If you condition yourself to say that it is too difficult to attempt or complete, you have already lost the battle. How you see and feel about the world is a replica of you, it is like looking in the mirror. Scientifically, humans can't fly but we sure can have a bird's eye view; be a problem solver and not a problem maker. Even when others don't see or believe in your vision don't join in because now the battle becomes you and others against yourself. If someone else doesn't believe in you, let that be their weakness or problem, not yours, that's their burden to bear.

Inhale confidence, exhale doubt - Unknown

Today's Affirmation:

_____

_____

_____

_____

_____

_____

_____

_____

_____

Evening Reflection:

_____

_____

_____

_____

_____

_____

_____

_____

_____

DAY 9

If you can't change the people around you....change the people around you! –Author Unknown

If you play with dirty dogs, there's a high possibility that you will catch fleas. But if you clean those dogs there's a possibility that everyone will avoid fleas. The people you surround yourself with have a major impact on your view of life and as a result, speaks volume on the way you are perceived. This world doesn't have time to dissect the various levels of your friendship or association therefore we are all branded according to the company we keep. Be sure to associate yourself with people who exude growth and grow with them, because you don't want to be left behind.

There's just one way to radically change your behaviour: radically change your environment. - Dr. B.J. Fogg

Today's Affirmation:

_____

_____

_____

_____

_____

_____

_____

_____

_____

Evening Reflection:

_____

_____

_____

_____

_____

_____

_____

_____

_____

DAY 10

You can change or simply change your point-of-view.

These two (2) phrases have the same meaning but the brain will react differently to both. Is the glass half-full or half-empty? Do you have a problem or do you need a solution? Your brain will recognize negative words such as "can't, won't and not" so remove them from your vocabulary and be strategic in the way you address situations. My mom would often quote Francis Bacon "If the mountain will not come to Muhammad, then Muhammad must go to the mountain". If things aren't going the way you anticipate, simply change your tactics.

You have to change the world or be changed by the world
- Tupac Shakur

Today's Affirmation:

_____

_____

_____

_____

_____

_____

_____

_____

_____

_____

Evening Reflection:

_____

_____

_____

_____

_____

_____

_____

_____

_____

_____

DAY 11

Be deliberate with your affirmations.

If you need a $1 mil, would you ask for $1K? It's the same thing with your affirmations! Whatever you need for your personal, academic, or professional growth it is mandatory to declare and decree the specifics. Sometimes affirmations aren't as clear as we expect them to be, that's why it is so important to know your worth to figure out the things that will enhance your growth. In some cases, people won't see your value, but that's okay because you don't have to share everything but be sure to write it down, speak it into existence and work your butt off.

To believe something is possible is to make it true.
- Friedrich Hebbel

Today's Affirmation:

_____

_____

_____

_____

_____

_____

_____

_____

_____

Evening Reflection:

_____

_____

_____

_____

_____

_____

_____

_____

_____

DAY 12

Become your own Rosa Parks and be a rebel for your future

Regardless of your age, there's a goal or few that you want to accomplish. So what are you waiting for? You need to put in the work, fight the distractions, create a game plan, and execute! Quit allowing others to determine your seat on the bus and become the bus driver. Control your destination by carving out your road map because only you should determine when to accelerate, slow down, or press those brakes.

Take back all control without remorse or regret.

Today's Affirmation:

_____

_____

_____

_____

_____

_____

_____

_____

_____

Evening Reflection:

_____

_____

_____

_____

_____

_____

_____

_____

_____

DAY 13

We are taught to be patient because God has a plan. However, you have to be willing to push through barriers, break down doors, and demand what's yours.

Be patient enough to trust the process but be more committed to pushing forward. You need to become so laser-focused that you envision result before you even start your task. Your journey will not be a straight road; there will be obstacles, failures, and setbacks but keep ploughing through the dirt because the fruit will be ready for harvest at the right time!

James 2:26 encapsulates that *"Faith without works is dead"*.

Today's Affirmation:

_____

_____

_____

_____

_____

_____

_____

_____

_____

Evening Reflection:

_____

_____

_____

_____

_____

_____

_____

_____

_____

_____

DAY 14

The easiest way to do nothing wrong; is to do nothing

Start that project!

Quit that job!

Leave that relationship!

Move up and on!

Don't become so comfortable with an uncomfortable environment that you don't realize that it is too toxic for you to excel. No one said it will be easy or be handed to you on a silver platter but it will be worth it. Be confident in your abilities to succeed and half the job is done.

Put on your cape and save yourself!

Today's Affirmation:

_____

_____

_____

_____

_____

_____

_____

_____

_____

Evening Reflection:

_____

_____

_____

_____

_____

_____

_____

_____

_____

DAY 15

To prepare for a marathon you will need to build stamina but 10-minute jogs won't cut it.

You've spent so much time in the infant stage just to realize your goals. You expect that there will be a smooth road ahead with no potholes or detours then suddenly obstacles arrive. You have to remain calm, recalculate a new path, and simply navigate through the terrains. This is your opportunity to endure and grow because that's the only way you handle difficult situations. Now you are truly ready for the uphill battle ahead. The marathon is not for the swift ONLY but for those who are swift and can endure to the end.

The Marathon Continues (TMC) - Nipsey Hussle

Today's Affirmation:

_____

_____

_____

_____

_____

_____

_____

_____

_____

_____

Evening Reflection:

_____

_____

_____

_____

_____

_____

_____

_____

_____

_____

DAY 16

*When you decide it is time to make a move,
be certain its not backwards.*

There's a vast difference between stepping back to analyze a scenario and going back to a negative situation. When we are on the pursuit of temporary happiness, love, or comfort; we tend to revisit familiar places or people that shelter us from shame or judgement. That can be very damaging because you can't heal in the place where you were hurt, so step back and analyze. Just don't go backward.

Even though life can be understood looking backward, it must be lived forwards- Inspired by Soren Kierkegaard

Today's Affirmation:

_____
_____
_____
_____
_____
_____
_____
_____
_____

Evening Reflection:

_____
_____
_____
_____
_____
_____
_____
_____
_____

DAY 17

Don't allow fear to paralyze you because the adrenaline rush will give you the strength you need.- Lori Deschene

Nothing beats a failure but a try. Don't give up on your first sign of struggle or failure; stumbling blocks will come but if you are truly passionate and commit to the process you will find a way. I just need you to finish what you've started, you may feel confused and frustrated but that's okay. Fight through the mental paralysis! Take a different approach if you have to, but don't quit in the pursuit of greatness. Continue to plough through the dirt until you find that diamond; that's what you call determination.

It's okay to struggle, but it's never okay to give up on yourself - John Zickfoose

Today's Affirmation:

_____

_____

_____

_____

_____

_____

_____

_____

_____

_____

Evening Reflection:

_____

_____

_____

_____

_____

_____

_____

_____

_____

_____

_____

DAY 18

I am not a failure but sometimes I fail!

You all fall short sometimes! Don't focus too much on the failure, your goal is to understand why you failed and what that failure has taught you. There was a lesson in that failed attempt, your responsibility is to learn from it. You owe it to your unwise and immature self.

Ask yourself these questions to truly grasp the reasoning behind that failed attempt:

Did I learn?

What did I learn?

Am I wiser?

How will my failures define my future successes?

Can my failure help someone else?

Today's Affirmation:

_____

_____

_____

_____

_____

_____

_____

_____

_____

Evening Reflection:

_____

_____

_____

_____

_____

_____

_____

_____

_____

DAY 19

Call me Victoria/ Victorious just not a victim!

Yes, your past experiences may have helped define you. After all; your environment shapes your behaviour. This battle called life will chew you up and spit you out but you have the will power to win the war. Stop letting bad experiences and bad people make you believe that you are a failure, your reaction should be to fight back 10 times harder. Dr. Maraboli said "Stop validating your victim mentality. Shake off your self-defeating drama and embrace your innate ability to recover and achieve." Even if it means you have to lose a few battles, the war is yours and the end will be sweet.

A victim mentality is a loser mindset!

Today's Affirmation:

_____

_____

_____

_____

_____

_____

_____

_____

_____

Evening Reflection:

_____

_____

_____

_____

_____

_____

_____

_____

_____

DAY 20

Don't be a slave to your pride.

It is remarkable when you are independent, knowledgeable, and strong. On the other hand, it is unimpressive when you are too independent, knowledgeable, and strong . Don't be so prideful that you find it difficult to ask for help, at some point we are all ignorant: spiritually, financially, and mentally and that's okay! If you have a solid tribe you won't feel inadequate because they know your failure is a burden to the entire team. Remember you will only be the weakest link until your team strengthens you.

Pride comes before destruction, and an arrogant spirit *before a fall.* Proverbs 16:18

Today's Affirmation:

_____

_____

_____

_____

_____

_____

_____

_____

_____

_____

Evening Reflection:

_____

_____

_____

_____

_____

_____

_____

_____

_____

_____

DAY 21

As God continues to reward you for your hard work,
be mindful of your arrogance because it can
block your blessings.

Have you been praying for your version of a miracle and as soon as you get it, you felt like you were invincible and started acting a fool? Many times we take 10 steps forward and an act of arrogance forces us 20 times backward. This usually happens when we disregard that there is a higher being guiding us towards victory. Don't be crippled by ignorance; remember to always stay humble, give gratitude to God, and watch your blessings multiply. Remember there's no place in your growth for egotism!

Gratitude is a must!

Blessings we ah reap pon we course in a handful

Wi nuh rise and boast

Yeah we give thanks like we need it the most

We haffi give thanks like we really supposed to be thankful!
- Koffee

Today's Affirmation:

_____

_____

_____

_____

_____

_____

_____

_____

_____

_____

Evening Reflection:

_____

_____

_____

_____

_____

_____

_____

_____

_____

_____

DAY 22

A real woman is defined as whatever the f@$k she wants to be! - Unknown

So what! You may or may not have children or a husband. You are not defined by your reproductive organs or a ring on your finger. YOU STRUT IN BEAST MODE. Who made them the judge, jury, and executioner of your femininity? If they think you can be defined by their opinions they are in for a rude awakening, you can't be defined by opinions. Avoid putting yourself through all that BS and live your life for you and drown out the noise! Can you picture yourself living to reach and please others and their standards? If you can, then you are living for others. You might as well give them your husband, salary, and the deed to your house as well as your inheritance. Now I'll ask you the same question. Can you still picture it? That's what I thought!

Live unapologetically!

Today's Affirmation:

_____

_____

_____

_____

_____

_____

_____

_____

_____

Evening Reflection:

_____

_____

_____

_____

_____

_____

_____

_____

_____

_____

DAY 23

*Maybe you can take the fruit but you won't
distort the root. She is grounded!*

We've all dated someone's immature son/ daughter who wasn't ready for our awesomeness! They've taken and taken with no regard or remorse for your Queendom. Even though it is not right it will be okay because you've covered your internal scars (heartbreak), mend that brittle organ (heart), and glistened with every touch of moisture (tears)! Through all this turmoil you've somehow remained loyal, committed, and brave which is the true testament to your integrity and upbringing.

They took the dragon fruit but you are the cactus!

Today's Affirmation:

_____

_____

_____

_____

_____

_____

_____

_____

_____

Evening Reflection:

_____

_____

_____

_____

_____

_____

_____

_____

_____

DAY 24

My Queen! Don't be confused, attention is ONLY temporary but respect is lasting.

People lie, cheat, and steal but the worst self-inflicting crime is losing who you are just to please others. No amount of followers, likes or mentions without self-value and self-respect means anything. As long as you respect yourself anyone who comes into contact with you will be forced to do the same. Even if they don't like you they will have to respect you.

You are the Queen of your Queendom even if there's no King for the Kingdom.

Today's Affirmation:

_____

_____

_____

_____

_____

_____

_____

_____

_____

Evening Reflection:

_____

_____

_____

_____

_____

_____

_____

_____

_____

DAY 25

We need to escape the faux-reality that has lead
to comparison and jealousy.

Like most things in life, too much indulging makes it a bad habit or addiction; be sure to take breaks and operate within moderation. Even though social media has made us somewhat anti-social it has also created this false sense of perfection. These things lead to jealousy and record levels of unhappiness. You have to take breaks from these filters and edit your focus on the reality of your life. Don't be consumed with comparing yourself to others or what they have, if it is yours nothing can prevent it from reaching you. Simply slay in your lane.

The grass is not always greener on the other side, it's a filter!

Today's Affirmation:

_____

_____

_____

_____

_____

_____

_____

_____

_____

Evening Reflection:

_____

_____

_____

_____

_____

_____

_____

_____

_____

DAY 26

*If you fix a crown, it is not your place to broadcast it.
Allow that King/ Queen to tell their own story.*

We need to know our place! There's no prize or glory for helping others then broadcasting it, as a matter of fact, it is disgusting and rude. Let your assistance be genuine and not self-serving. You will quickly realize that if you help others just to make yourself feel good, you will become a fixer rather than a friend. Help others because they need it not because your ego or self-righteous spirit is hungry.

Be a friend, not a fixer!

Today's Affirmation:

_____

_____

_____

_____

_____

_____

_____

_____

_____

_____

Evening Reflection:

_____

_____

_____

_____

_____

_____

_____

_____

_____

_____

DAY 27

Every time you repeat the gossip, you join the gossip.

Yesterday we spoke about telling other people's story, I believe its important to revisit this from the other side of the spectrum. Before you even repeat what you heard ask yourself these questions:

Was the source reliable?

Is it even true?

Would it hurt him/her?

How does it benefit me?

Remember, everything that is given to you is not for consumption or reproduction. Get out of the habit of over-sharing cancers because there's no cure!

Today's Affirmation:

_____

_____

_____

_____

_____

_____

_____

_____

_____

Evening Reflection:

_____

_____

_____

_____

_____

_____

_____

_____

_____

DAY 28

As time passes, pain becomes a memory-Unknown Author

Avoid being hell-bent on the wrong or shame that someone has caused you. It takes much more mental space and energy to be angry with someone rather than simply forgiving him/her. The average brain weighs around 3 pounds, do you want to clog your 3 pounds with animosity or revenge? Forgive them so you can bloom like a rose because forgiveness is for your growth and healing. Remove those mental shackles and allow your creativity to flow like a river; free of judgement and scorn.

Your temporary breakdown becomes a permanent breakthrough.

Today's Affirmation:

_____

_____

_____

_____

_____

_____

_____

_____

_____

Evening Reflection:

_____

_____

_____

_____

_____

_____

_____

_____

_____

DAY 29

My future will be better than in my past!

Now that you are more aware of the crippling mindset that can stunt your growth, this is the perfect time to adjust your current decisions to enhance your future results. The past is simply what it is, the past, your weight has been lifted and your spirit shall be free of burden. Use the rest of your life to enjoy your life and continuously improve your mindset. This is where it starts, the rebirth of a legend!

The distinction between the past, present, and future is only a stubbornly persistent illusion. - Albert Einstein

Today's Affirmation:

_____

_____

_____

_____

_____

_____

_____

_____

_____

Evening Reflection:

_____

_____

_____

_____

_____

_____

_____

_____

_____

DAY 30

I am committed to this rebirth and my legacy continues!

Letter to the old Your Name   dd/mm/yy

_____

_____

_____

_____

_____

_____

_____

_____

_____

_____

_____

_____

_____

_____

_____

_____

_____

_____

_____

Letter to the old Your Name   dd/mm/yy

_____

_____

_____

_____

_____

_____

_____

_____

_____

_____

_____

_____

_____

_____

_____

_____

_____

_____

_____

_____

_____

Made in the USA
Coppell, TX
23 November 2020